# INANIMATE

## Nick Robideau

**BROADWAY PLAY PUBLISHING INC**
New York
www.broadwayplaypub.com
info@broadwayplaypub.com

INANIMATE
© Copyright 2020 Nick Robideau

Cover image by Eleanor Philips

First edition: November 2020
I S B N: 978-0-88145-879-4

Book design: Marie Donovan
Page make-up: Adobe InDesign
Typeface: Palatino

The World Premiere of INANIMATE was produced by The Flea Theater (Niegel Smith, Artistic Director; Carol Ostrow, Producing Director) in New York, running from 21 August-24 September 2017. The cast and creative contributors were:

ERICA .................................................................Lacy Allen
KEVIN..............................................................Maki Borden
DEE........................................................... Philip Feldman
TRISH..........................................................Tressa Preston
CHORUS 1 ...................................................Artem Kreimer
CHORUS 2 ................................... Nancy Tatiana Quintana
CHORUS 3 ................................................Michael Oloyede

*Understudies:*
CHORUS 1 ...................................... Marcus Antonio Jones
CHORUS 2 ................................................ Alexandra Slater

*Director*......................................................Courtney Ulrich
*Scenic design*.............................................. Yu-Hsuan Chen
*Costume design*.......................................... Sarah Lawrence
*Lighting design* .............................Becky Heisler McCarthy
*Sound design*....................................................Megan Culley
*Assistant director*........................................Claire Edmonds
*Production stage manager* .............................. Gina Solebello

# CHARACTERS & SETTING

ERICA GRILLO, *30.*

TRISH GRILLO, *mid-30s.* ERICA's *sister.*

KEVIN RUSSELL, *30.* ERICA's *classmate from kindergarten right through to the end of high school. They casually know each other in the way that all small-town people who grew up together (but didn't necessary socialize) do.*

DEE, *younger but no specific age.* ERICA's *new love interest. The strong, silent type. Mysterious and enigmatic.*

*The rest of the cast is made up of a chorus of 2M, 1W. Throughout the play they portray various inanimate objects and townspeople.*

*On doubling:* DEE *can be folded into the* CHORUS, *reducing the total cast size to 3M, 3W. It's also possible to have one* CHORUS *play the inanimate objects and a second* CHORUS *of two men and one woman play the human characters, bringing the total cast up to 10: 6M, 4W*

*A small, blue-collar town in Massachusetts*

*Time: The present*

(ERICA, *alone by a Dairy Queen sign*)

ERICA: I have two images of my face
In my mind
The first one's like this:
*(She scrunches her face up in a sour expression.)*
That's my "before" face
Or my "before you" face
I guess is what I mean
I don't have the actual expression memorized
It's not like I was staring into the mirror
But it must've been terrible
*(Who is she talking to? Nobody? The sky? It's not clear.)*
And it felt like my heart was doing the same thing
Like my face and heart were directly connected in
some way
All tight and scrunched in unison
I'd see someone laughing
Or talking really fast in that way people do when they
get excited
Or singing along to the radio, and I'd think...
I wonder what that feels like
It was like being slightly out of sync with the rest of the
world
And it was like that for so long
But now
Now
My face is like this:
*(She tilts her head up and offers a pleasant, neutral face.)*

It unscrunched
And my heart unscrunched with it
And I realized…
This is what it's like to feel alive
This is what it's like to feel *anything*
You did that
You unscrunched me
And the thing is
Okay
The thing is
I love you.
And it's so crazy and weird and exciting and scary for
me to admit that
To actually say it out loud
But now I have
And…say something?

*(DEE enters.)*

DEE: Look up at me
Looking down on you
And as the light caresses your face
Its warm glow mirrors your heart

ERICA: That's…wow
I mean, I thought you felt the same way
But I didn't want to assume or anything
The whole world feels different now
Nothing's ever going to be the same, is it?

*(The CHORUS enters. We are in a grocery store.)*

CHORUS 1: Two plies, quilted
Straining under
A clear shiny skin
Squeeze me!

ERICA: Noble utility
I really admire that

I bet you're really soft

CHORUS 2: Pliable plastic
Sloshing white
The glug of a hello
Farm fresh!

ERICA: Does my face look different to you?

Stupid question
You've never seen me before
But does my face look nice?
It feels nice
Am I smiling?
I think I might be.

CHORUS 2: I let a bead of condensation roll onto your
hand

ERICA: Thanks
It helps to have confirmation
I like how wet you are
It feels like dew
And I...
Am I talking out loud?
I am
I'm talking out loud
You know what?
Who cares!
I'm not taking this back
I am NOT taking this back

CHORUS 3: Black rubber
Cold metal
Feel the contrast on your skin

ERICA: Hello. Aren't you a cutie?

CHORUS 3: Oxo Good Grip
Non-slip

Satisfaction guaranteed.

ERICA: That's nice
I like a guarantee
And you're...
But I'm in love
I know we just met
But I just want to tell everyone, you know?
I'm in love

CHORUS 3: Feel the way I move
So smoothly
Open, closed

ERICA: Well, as long as we're clear
You are...beautiful
Open, closed.

CHORUS 1: What seems to be the problem?

CHORUS 2: That. That's the problem.

*(CHORUS 3 exits. CHORUS 1 and 2 become the Manager and the CUSTOMER. ERICA is wearing a supermarket employee's uniform and standing at a cash register. She holds a can opener in her hand and talks to it.)*

CHORUS 1/MANAGER: Erica?

ERICA: Open, closed
That's really nice

CHORUS 2/CUSTOMER: She's just been...talking. To the groceries.

ERICA: Open, closed
It's a little like breathing

MANAGER: Miss Grillo!

CUSTOMER: As in...Trish Grillo's kid sister? Shit. These politicians and their dirty little secrets, am I right?

ERICA: Isn't it kind of amazing?

Before, I would have just let you pass right by
I wouldn't have dared....

*(The* MANAGER *strides over and snatches the can opener out
of* ERICA's *hand.)*

MANAGER: What are you *doing*, Erica?

*(*ERICA *hesitates.)*

CUSTOMER: I tell you what she was doing. She was
talkin' to the freakin' groceries. And she put that can
opener down her...her shirt! Don't think I didn't see
that, you frickin sicko.

MANAGER: Erica?

ERICA: They...um. They talked to me first.

MANAGER: Okay. That's. And the can opener, down
your... *(He shudders.)*

ERICA: I got a little carried away. I'm sorry. You're, um,
always saying I need to be friendlier at checkout, right?

MANAGER: To the *customers*! Not to...to...*can openers!*

ERICA: Here's the thing, Bill. I—

MANAGER: You know what? I don't care. In fact, you're
fired.

ERICA: But I—

MANAGER: Ma'am, why don't we set you up with some
store credit for your trouble?

CUSTOMER: How much store credit we talkin'?

MANAGER: Let's step into my office to discuss things
further. And Erica...I expect you to be gone when I get
back. *(Exits)*

CUSTOMER: Freak.

*(The* CUSTOMER *smiles sweetly, and follows the* MANAGER
*off.* ERICA *turns to exit and notices the can opener, still
sitting at her now-former register.)*

ERICA: Open, closed…
*(She quickly picks up the can opener.)*
Hello again.

*(DEE enters.)*

ERICA: Freak
That's what she called me
Freak

DEE: Hear the hum of my electricity
Just a little softer than usual
A little gentler
Feel that softness
In your bones

ERICA: I mean, I didn't expect them to high-five me
I knew they might not understand
But I wasn't ready for their faces
For their eyes

DEE: Look, I'm casting shadows
On you
One shadow, right there
Tracing a finger of dark across your face

ERICA: I do feel safe with you, always
None of this changes that
But…I just can't do that again
"Freak…"
I just can't believe that
But if I have to keep hearing it
Then we will be poisoned
Do you understand that?
It's psychological pollution

DEE: A little surge of power

Makes a mini crescendo
Music in a minor key

Meant just for you.

(DEE *exits.* ERICA *is alone with the actual Dairy Queen sign, which she directly addresses.*)

ERICA: Thank you, for understanding
And I know it hurts
But I can feel you, I really see you
I know how beautiful you are
And all anyone else can see is…
The Dairy Queen sign
Nothing can cure that kind of blindness
What I'm trying to say is…
Maybe I was wrong
About saying it out loud, at least
I am NOT taking it back
Not between you and me
But I think from now on…
We have to be a secret
And I have to be a secret
But secrets can be beautiful, right?
They're something too fragile to share with the world
And I still—

KEVIN: *(Voice only)* Erica?
(*He emerges from the shadows. He wears a Dairy Queen uniform.*)

ERICA: Kevin?

KEVIN: Who're you talking to?

ERICA: Nobody—well, I mean—

KEVIN: No, I get it. Stupid question. I talk to myself on the regular.

ERICA: What're you doing here?

(KEVIN *points to his uniform.*)

KEVIN: I don't wear this shit as a fashion statement.

ERICA: But it's late.

KEVIN: Annual inventory…which, I might add, Julie sprang on me, like, yesterday. And she knows full well that Thursday is my D & D night.

(ERICA *gives* KEVIN *a quizzical look.*)

KEVIN: You know. Dungeons and Dragons. Elves. Hobgoblins. Mystical quests of adventure. Twenty-sided die. You really don't—nevermind.

(ERICA *isn't really listening. She's somewhere else.*)

KEVIN: I'm supposed to be DMing right now. That's, like, coming up with the adventure. It's like writing a choose your own adventure story. And I had so much cool shit planned. Ugh. Anyhow, we had to cancel the whole thing. Because I'm here. And Julie just—
(*He suddenly realizes that something's up with her.*)
Um. Are you okay?

(ERICA *looks at* KEVIN.)

ERICA: No. I don't think so.

KEVIN: What's up?

ERICA: I…it's, um, hard to explain.

KEVIN: You're pregnant.

(ERICA *makes a face.*)

KEVIN: Oh God. I was kidding, but, I mean—

ERICA: No! I'm not…that's not it.

KEVIN: Then…what?

(ERICA *quickly looks at* KEVIN, *then shakes her head.*)

KEVIN: I did think it was a little weird when you didn't come in this afternoon. I mean, you're pretty much my best customer…so…you do know we're closed, right?

ERICA: I just need to get my shit together. I have to…to breathe.

KEVIN: So you came to the DQ? Seems like an odd choice of venue for clearing one's head.

ERICA: I just like it here.

KEVIN: Okay, well...whatever the reason may be, I'm here for you. I mean it. Clearly you came here of all places for a reason, and—

ERICA: I got fired. Okay? I got fired.

KEVIN: Oh man. Erica. I'm so...that really sucks. I can't even—I mean, the year you're having, I'm sorry.

ERICA: That job was the only thing that made me feel like a real person.

KEVIN: I refuse to believe that. You're better than that place.

ERICA: No. I wasn't.

KEVIN: What the hell happened? If you don't mind my asking?

ERICA: I...

KEVIN: I get the sense that you do, in fact, mind my asking.

ERICA: We just...we barely even know each other. No offense, but this is—

KEVIN: Do six months of daily Blizzards mean nothing to you?

ERICA: That was—

KEVIN: And homeroom for four years. Mr. Martinson's English class. Gym. Shit, *gym*, Erica!

We barely know each other? I don't even...honestly, I think I'm mildly to moderately offended. And it's not like I haven't tried. May I remind you that you declined at least a dozen invites to King Richard's Faire? And like, I get it, Renaissance fairs are corny or whatever, but The Madrigals have been really on point

lately, if I do say so myself. I finally nailed the tenor
part on Agincourt Carol last Saturday. I think you
would've—

ERICA: I'm sorry, okay? I...I'm sorry I didn't go see
your singing group. I'm sure you were great. I'm sorry.
I'm sorry.

KEVIN: Hey. Hey. It's cool. This isn't about me. I
shouldn't have run my mouth. You have my full
permission, at any time, to say "Shut up, Kevin", OK?
I need that sometimes. This is about you right now.
You're having a really bad night. How can I help?

ERICA: *(Quickly)* Get me a job.

KEVIN: Um, for real?

ERICA: You're practically a manager, right? And it
would really help...I mean, my sister's going to be
pissed off. I'm still not paying her anything for rent,
so...but if I had something else lined up. So you
could...I mean, if you wouldn't mind....

KEVIN: Okay. Okay. Well Trent just got a gig at Barnes
and Noble...the asshole thinks he's really hot shit
now...and that means we have a spot to fill. Erica,
serious question. Are you fucking with me right now?

ERICA: I'm not fucking with you. I swear.

KEVIN: Then...okay. Cool. Yeah. I think we can make
this happen.

ERICA: Really?

KEVIN: Really. Congratulations, I guess, future ice
cream slinger of America.

ERICA: Thanks, I...thanks, Kevin. Really.

KEVIN: Don't mention it. Or...do. If you want...or, I
guess what I'm trying to say is you're welcome.

ERICA: Well, I should…my sister just gets kind of weird if I—

KEVIN: Yeah. Sure. Of course.

(ERICA *turns, looks up at the sign, and begins to exit.*)

KEVIN: Hey.

(ERICA *stops.*)

ERICA: What?

KEVIN: You really, truly like it here?

ERICA: Yeah. I do.

KEVIN: Why? I mean, it's just some crappy Dairy Queen.

ERICA: I just…do.

(KEVIN *considers this.*)

KEVIN: Cool. Goodnight, Erica…

(KEVIN *exits.* ERICA *follows. The scene shifts to a small bedroom in a modest, middle-class home. She picks up a television remote, presses the power button, and looks out at the audience as she watches the unseen T V.*)

T V VOICE: You're watching Channel 47, Blackstone Valley Cable Access. Don't just watch T V…make it. (*Cheesy theme music plays. Maybe some kind of low-budget opening credits. Upstage of* ERICA, *a curtain or flat depicting a cable access set appears.*)
And now, coming to you live from the municipal library's media room, it's *Talk of the Town*, with Frank Holden!

(*Theme music plays again.* FRANK *enters. He is supremely corny.*)

FRANK: Welcome to *Talk of the Town*, your nightly round-up of all the local news that's fit to print, plus sometimes a little that's not (*he chuckles to himself*). As always, if you have something to say, the lines are open, just call 800-555-47473. That's 800-555-GRIPE.

First up, we're very happy to welcome back to the program, Selectwoman Trish Grillo.She's been teasing it for weeks now, but I'm just tickled pink that she's offered Talk of the Town the exclusive scoop: brand new details for Ballot Question 6, The Downtown Revitalization Project. Trish, come on out.

*(Theme music plays again.* TRISH, *mid-30s enters.)*

TRISH: Great to be here, Frank. And how are things up at the junior-senior high school? Not to speak out of school, as it were, but it seems like just yesterday Frank and I were getting detention for passing notes in bio. Now he's teaching the whole gosh-darn class! Wheredoes the time go?

FRANK: That's what I love about the life sciences. The kids may be Snapchatting these days instead of passing notes, but protein synthesis, much like detention, never goes out of style. *(He laughs a little)* But enough jibber jabber. I understand, Trish, that you have something you'd like to say.

TRISH: I do, Frank. I do.

FRANK: Then let's get right to it. The floor is yours.

TRISH: Thanks, Frank.
*(She stands, rather dramatically, and looks out, gravely.)*
Hello, friends. I'd like to dedicate this moment to my mother, the late, great Harriet McKinney. Her legacy as our Town Manager for fifteen wonderful years looms almost as large as what she considered to be her greatest accomplishment of all: being a single, working mother to me and my sister Erica.
As I watched her fierce, valiant two-year struggle against cancer come to an end last winter, I made a promise to her, and to myself: to continue her life's

work in any way I could. That's why I am so pleased
to reveal, *exclusively*, my vision for our new, revitalized
downtown.

FRANK: Sarah, could you pull up those renderings?

TRISH: Beautiful, isn't it?

FRANK: Mmm. Yes. But beautiful is expensive, Trish.
I've heard a lot of rumblings around the ole teachers'
lounge water cooler about what it's going to mean for
John and Jane Q Public. Care to comment?

TRISH: I've said it before, and I'll say it again: there will
be no tax increases.

FRANK: I read your financial proposal this morning.
There's a mention there about the power plants up on
Maple Street…?

TRISH: Yes. Frank, friends at home, I know many of
you weren't too happy when my mother approved
those power plants, but we're seeing the benefit of her
foresight now. The tax revenue from those very plants
will be more than enough to cover our costs.

FRANK: But Trish, if I may, it's more than just the
construction costs. In my own personal chats over
the proverbial garden fence, the grants seem to be
a real sticking point. Some might even call them a
government hand-out. Not me.

TRISH: Okay. Well. Let me remind you: this isn't Wal-
Mart or Home Depot we're talking about here. These
are your friends and neighbors.

FRANK: Returning to your proposal, you're estimating
that business owners who choose to opt in are looking
at closing for six-to-nine months.

TRISH: Exactly, Frank. That's why the grants are so
important. These small business owners are going to
need some help to make up for the lost revenue while

we tear down all those old downtown eyesores and build the beautiful new downtown core you see here. So this grant money isn't a handout. It's a lifeline for them. It's a lifeline for our town itself, in this very real fight against chain store oblivion.

FRANK: Well alright, let's go to the phone lines. Caller, you're live.

TRISH: Caller, hi, I hope you're having a lovely evening. I'm hoping that I can—

*(The* CUSTOMER *appears in a pool of light, talking on her cell phone.)*

CUSTOMER: Yeah, gotta say, I don't trust Trish. I mean, everyone knows that kid sister of hers is a freak. Heard all kinds of rumors about what goes on in that house of theirs. I don't care who their mother was, that's not the kind of family I want to trust with our town's future.

TRISH: Frank, clearly this is some kind of crank call. If we could just—

FRANK: Caller, care to explain yourself?

CUSTOMER: Gladly. I was at her sister's checkout line at the Market Basket yesterday and she was having some kinda, I dunno, mental breakdown. She had a can opener, down her…her shirt. Just rubbing it on her boobs and moaning and stuff. In front of everyone! And there were children there! It was…pornographic.

ERICA: Shit…

TRISH: Frank, this is the first I'm hearing of this. But if it's true, I'll—

CUSTOMER: I mean, I heard she's a schizo or something like that.

ERICA: All I did was say hello. What's so wrong about that…?

TRISH: Now that's a little unfair, caller. I assure you, Erica is not crazy and she's certainly not schizophrenic. She's always been a little…unique…and—

CUSTOMER: Unique. Sure. Well I say take care of your own freakin' house before you even start thinking about this nonsense with our downtown.

(ERICA *turns off the T V and throws the remote.* FRANK, TRISH, *and the* CUSTOMER *exit, taking the cable access set with them.* ERICA *glares at the television for a moment, then takes the can opener out of her pocket and squeezes it tight. She pulls teddy bear out of a drawer or box, and turns on an old floor lamp.*)

ERICA: Hi. Are you…
Can you hear me?

*(After a moment the* CHORUS *enters.)*

CHORUS 1: I explode with light!
See the spots in your eyes?

ERICA: Yes. I'm here.
I'm really talking to you
And I'm really listening to you

CHORUS 2: My arms, feel!
So fluffy. So fuzzy.
So cold. So empty.
There, right there—that shape?
The memory of you.

ERICA: I promise not to ignore you ever again
I'm not going to ignore myself ever again
Because I need you
I hope you'll still let me need you

CHORUS 2: Warm fur! Cozy eyes!

CHORUS 1: A burst of shimmering!

ERICA: Thank you

CHORUS 3: Open, open, open

ERICA: Oh…everyone, this is Oxo
Oxo, everyone

CHORUS 3: A creak of an invitation

CHORUS 2: Little stitchy smile!
Trace the curve
Up up up!

CHORUS 1: A shadow shivers, wary

(*The objects look at each other, then turn to look at* ERICA, *expectantly.*)

ERICA: Oh, I…
I guess what I wanted to…
Am I crazy?
Please tell me I'm not crazy.

(CHORUS 2 *approaches* ERICA *and embraces her.*)

CHORUS 2: Squeeze me!

(CHORUS 1 *approaches* ERICA *and stares into her eyes.*)

CHORUS 1: See me.

(CHORUS 3 *approaches, takes* ERICA'*s hand, and caresses her palm.*)

CHORUS 3: Hear me
Know me

(*The* CHORUS *exits. Scene shifts back to the Dairy Queen parking lot.* ERICA *and* DEE, *together. Some kind of physical contact between them—affectionate. Peaceful. After a moment,* KEVIN *enters.*)

KEVIN: We have to stop meeting like this.

(DEE *exits.*)

ERICA: Oh. Hey.

KEVIN: You know you don't start until tomorrow, right?

ERICA: You saw the T V, right? Do I even still have a job?

KEVIN: Oh yeah. Julie's totally, completely desperate for help. No offense or anything.

ERICA: You must think I'm the biggest freak on the planet.

KEVIN: If I did, I would only count it as a good thing.

ERICA: I guess. What are you doing here?

KEVIN: Maybe I had a little inkling that you might stop by. Seems like you make it kind of a habit of coming by after hours.

ERICA: Well, um, it's just…the sign. It's really pretty all lit up at night.

KEVIN: Whatever you say….

ERICA: What I mean is…um…I'm a little nervous about tomorrow.

KEVIN: Trust me, there is *nothing* to be nervous about. fifteen year-olds do that shit on a regular basis.

ERICA: But I don't. I'm just afraid I'll…screw it up.

KEVIN: Well how 'bout we practice?

ERICA: I mean, you already locked up, and—

(KEVIN *takes out his wallet.*)

KEVIN: Okay. This wallet is the ice cream cone. And the machine…the machine is here.
(*He indicates the empty air in front of him.*)
See it?

ERICA: I guess so.

KEVIN: And the lever is right here
(*He pulls on the imaginary lever.*)

ERICA: Okay. Got it.

KEVIN: Now, the proper operation of the soft serve machine is a task that requires skill, talent, and tenacity. Bottom line, Julie flips her shit if it's not done right.

ERICA: Um. This is not helping me feel less nervous.

KEVIN: Hey. Stick with me, kid, and you'll be a star. Julie won't know what hit her. Now, observe the master at work.

*(He mimes filling the "cone" with "ice cream".)*

ERICA: Very…masterful.

KEVIN: Well come on, let's see what you're made of.

*(ERICA mimes filling a cone with ice cream. KEVIN makes a buzzer sound [as in "incorrect!"].)*

KEVIN: I'm gonna stop you right there. Where's the signature twist, rookie?

*(ERICA throws the wallet down in frustration.)*

KEVIN: Hey. Hang on. Don't despair. It's just one motion in the wrist. Master this, and you'll be golden tomorrow. Julie will think you're some kind of prodigy.

*(KEVIN stands behind ERICA and guides her hands. He sings a few bars of* Unchained Melody.*)*

KEVIN: Y'know. *Ghost.* The whole thing with the…. nevermind.

ERICA: Like…that?

KEVIN: Stupendous. A round of applause for the brash young upstart, Miss Erica Grillo…

*(KEVIN lets his hands linger on ERICA's, and continues to hold her from behind, even though the lesson is over.)*

ERICA: Thank you so much, Kevin. For being cool.
These last couple days have just been...and, well
you've been—

(KEVIN *kisses* ERICA. *She pulls away. He looks at her, and
panics.*)

KEVIN: Shit. Shit! Sorry. I didn't mean to—

ERICA: Um....

KEVIN: Sorry, I was getting some vibes, and...shit.
There aren't, in fact, any vibes here, are there?

ERICA: You just...I mean—aren't you gay?

KEVIN: Oh Jesus Christ.

ERICA: It's just—you and Tommy Belliveau. You two
were...you know.

KEVIN: God. How do you know about that?

ERICA: Tracey Gasper and Megan Carey were talking
about it in the break room, and they—

KEVIN: This shit has reached the Market Basket break
room?

ERICA: Sorry.

KEVIN: And this is why I make it a policy not to date
anyone who lives within a ten-mile radius of this town.
Or that's the policy for guys at least. Fucking Tommy.
I knew that was a bad idea. But...okay, did you know
he's this really amazing glass blower? The Madrigals
performed right next to his booth at King Richard's
Faire all season this year. Not to be too much of a perv
about it, but if you had seen what he could do with
molten glass...

ERICA: Yeah. Totally. So...you're bi?

KEVIN: That word is so 1998. I'm not exactly into labels.
They're limiting.

ERICA: Right. I mean...I agree. Completely.

*(Weird silence, again.* ERICA *and* KEVIN *both hesitate, unsure of what to say.)*

ERICA: I should really get back. Big day tomorrow, right?

KEVIN: Well. I fucked this up, didn't I?

ERICA: Oh, no, hey, I mean, I, uh…

KEVIN: You said you have to go. I don't want to… keep you or anything. I've already…but could you do me a favor? I know it's stupid and lame, but…

ERICA: What?

KEVIN: Could you say happy birthday? Nobody else has. I take that back. My dad texted me, which I feel like sort of doesn't count. I just thought it might be cool to hear the words before midnight…

ERICA: Oh, um…I didn't…happy birthday?

KEVIN: The big three-oh. You know how I spent it? Cleaning puke out of the men's room. At Dairy Queen. Where I have worked since I was seventeen.

*(His voice quivers.)*

You wanna hear the dumbest shit ever? Last April, one of the guys from D & D, his roommate moved in with his girlfriend, and he asked me to take the room. In Waltham, which is a cool enough place, I guess. It's not here, right? And it would have been a stretch, but I could have managed the rent. But I…I hesitated. I don't know why. I just…I should have said yes. Right away. But he asked somebody else. So I'm still here. And it's all I can think about. I had my shot. And I blew it.
*(He is actually crying now.)*
You ever feel like you can't breathe? Like, someone or something is for real pushing down on your chest? And like everything inside if you is just saying run…

run…run…who the fuck even knows where. Just go. Because you're going to die. Ever feel like that?

(ERICA, *frozen in place, does not respond.* KEVIN *collects himself.*)

KEVIN: I shouldn't have tried to kiss you. That was stupid and pathetic and…and I'm sorry I made a sexual innuendo about Tommy and glass-blowing. That was totally embarrassing and inappropriate. I just say shit without thinking sometimes. Just forget it. Forget about all of it. I'll see you tomorrow, okay? I'm sorry.

(ERICA *raises her arms, in a strange approximation of an invitation to a hug.* KEVIN *trails off. They look at each other.*)

ERICA: This is sort of weird for me. I mean, I don't hug, pretty much as a rule. So if you don't want to, I'll just put my arms down, and…

(KEVIN *awkwardly walks into* ERICA's *embrace.*)

ERICA: Thirty's rough. On my…day, I guess…last month, my sister took me to Red Robin. It was just the two of us and for some reason her receptionist from the real estate office, who I think she had to bribe to be there, and…that was kind of depressing.

KEVIN: It's not quite Dairy Queen men's room barf, but I'll give you a close second. Not that it's some kind of misery competition or anything.

(ERICA *looks over* KEVIN's *shoulder and up at the Dairy Queen sign. They hold the embrace for a silent moment. He looks her in the eyes. She cannot hold his gaze, and pulls away.*)

ERICA: I…I gotta go.

KEVIN: Right now?

ERICA: Yeah. Sorry, I…happy birthday, Kevin.

(ERICA *exits quickly.* KEVIN *is completely and totally alone. He stares off in the direction she went, then exits as well. The scene shifts to* TRISH *and* ERICA'*s house, the next night.* ERICA *re-enters and turns the T V on.* )

T V VOICE: You're watching Channel 47, Blackstone Valley Cable Access. Don't just watch TV…make it.

(TRISH *and* FRANK *enter with the* Talk of the Town *set.*)

FRANK: Welcome back to the show, Trish.

TRISH: Thrilled to be here, as always.

FRANK: Well, we had a record number of online comments after yesterday's program. To any new viewers joining us for the first time: welcome, and stay a while. I'm here to be *your* voice.

TRISH: I'm happy to answer any questions anyone might have. That's why I'm here.

(FRANK *takes out a phone and scrolls on it.*)

FRANK: Let's look at the official Talk of the Town Twitter feed. Ah! Twitter user @HotPartyChick69 says, "OMG, is that true about Trish's sister? Wicked gross." Hashtag Jerry Springer.

TRISH: I don't really see how that's…Frank, could we stick to questions about the downtown bill, please?

FRANK: The people want answers, Trish. And besides… hmm…yeah, most of the other tweets seem to be about yesterday's bombshell tip, exclusively reported right here on *Talk of the Town*. Okay…well, user @ DocJones45 says, "Nice pictures for the Downtown Project. Quaint." Oh, but there's a followup tweet here… "Not sure about all that sister stuff, though. Isn't crazy a genetic thing? What else is Trish hiding?" Hashtag Think of the Children, Hashtag Crazy Politicians…."

(FRANK *exits with the* Talk of the Town *set.* TRISH *crosses down to join* ERICA.)

TRISH: Hey you. How was the first day?

ERICA: There's this signature twist, right? And I think I really nailed it.

TRISH: Oh, that's great.

ERICA: I mean, my new boss said it was the best she's ever—

TRISH: You watch out for that Julie Mailette. You know she's been at every single selectmen's meeting this month, just fucking ranting that the D R P is some kind of conspiracy to bring her down? The Dairy Queen's not even inside the Downtown Business District. What does she care? But she always has to make it about her. Has since she was a teenager. Plus I'm pretty sure she blew my prom date behind the Getty station while we were waiting for the limo. Not that I care anymore. Ancient history, right?

ERICA: I dunno, it's like the third or fourth time you've brought it up since—

TRISH: Oh! Speaking of ancient history, you'll never guess who I talked to today.

ERICA: Dad?

TRISH: Very funny. Joey Arcand. You remember Joey, from high school?

ERICA: Sure. I remember the time he and Marc Spencer threatened to show up at the Gay-Straight Alliance meeting with baseball bats, and—

(TRISH *laughs, somewhat artificially.*)

TRISH: Boys, right? But come on, Erica. Seriously. He's a football player. I know you like to pretend you don't care about that stuff, but you have to admit, it's kind of sexy. A football player.

ERICA: Okay, first of all, he hasn't been a football player in twelve years. He's working for his dad's landscaping company these days, I think. And second—

TRISH: And from what he was saying, he's pretty goddamn depressed about it. So hey, the two of you have something in common!

ERICA: What did you do, Trish?

TRISH: And! And! I got you something. A present...
*(She rushes off and comes back with a little black dress, tags still on it.)*
I didn't want to go too far outside your comfort zone, so I went with black. Isn't it nice?

ERICA: I'm going to ask you again. What. Did. You. Do?

TRISH: I was getting to that! So what're you doing Friday night?

ERICA: No. No no no no no—

TRISH: Just give him a chance! He's really mellowed out these last few years. Well, since the D U I. He's not nearly as, you know, angry as he used to be.

ERICA: You can't just...just...spring something on me like this.

TRISH: It'll be great, trust me. I got you a nice table at Bertucci's. You love Bertucci's. And, you know, if you see any selectmen or members of the Downtown Business Alliance while you're there, just be polite. And introduce Joey.

ERICA: Okay. Yeah. I get it.

TRISH: No. Hey. It's not like—

ERICA: I embarrassed you. I'm sorry. I already apologized for that. And I'm sorry this town is such bullshit that people really might vote against your bill because your little sister is crazy or whatever. But I—

TRISH: Nobody thinks you're crazy.

ERICA: I'm not going to pretend to be something I'm not just to make you look good.

TRISH: How is going on a first date with a nice guy something you're not?

ERICA: Because it just…is.

TRISH: It's not just about, you know…politics.

ERICA: Sure it isn't.

TRISH: Erica, I say this with all the love in the world, but you kind of need to snap out of it.

ERICA: What's that supposed to mean?

TRISH: Well, you've sort of…regressed since Mom died.

ERICA: I don't know what you're talking about.

TRISH: You were always a loner or whatever. And hey, that's fine. You do you. But whatever you're doing now, this is something else. I don't get it.

ERICA: I haven't regressed. I haven't! Maybe I'm just taking this time to figure things out.

Maybe Mom being gone is, like, a chance in a weird way. To see things more clearly.

TRISH: See what things more clearly?

ERICA: It's…never mind.

TRISH: It's been seven months. You have to try to be around other people at some point.

ERICA: Ugh. I can't. I can't. I can't go out with Joey!

TRISH: Give me one reason why not.

ERICA: Because I…I…I'm seeing someone. And I think I'm in love.

TRISH: Oh. Well why didn't you tell me, you little shit? That's where you've been going at night, isn't it?

ERICA: Kinda, yeah.

TRISH: Well, who is it? Who's the lucky guy? Is it someone I know? Come on, spill.

(ERICA *thinks hard. In this moment, she seriously considers telling* TRISH *everything.*)

ERICA: Kevin. Kevin Russell.

TRISH: Kevin Russell from high school? Isn't he gay?

ERICA: No! Can't you just be happy for me?

TRISH: Fine. Yes. Congratulations. I really, truly am glad that you're not alone. Really.

ERICA: Thanks.

TRISH: Guess I should call Joey. It's probably for the best, him still being on probation and all. That'd probably put a damper on things. And hey, keep the dress. For your next night out with Kevin.

(TRISH *holds out the dress.* ERICA *hesitates, then takes it. She forces a smile.*)

TRISH: Well…'night, Erica.

ERICA: 'Night.

(TRISH *exits.*)

ERICA: I just…I just don't know…

(*The* CHORUS *enters.*)

ERICA: It's a matter of self-preservation, right?

Preserving me and Dee
Building a wall around us

CHORUS 1: I snap the light away
And you're back in the dark.

ERICA: I know, I get it
I almost did tell her
The truth, all of it.

There was this moment in the space between her
asking the question:
*Who is it?*
And me answering
In that space
I wasn't totally sure what I was going to say

CHORUS 2: Snuggles! Nuzzles!
So boneless-squishy!
Just. Like. You.

ERICA: It's not weakness, it's not
But you know her
You were hers before you were mine, after all
And she sees the world in a certain way
A way with absolutes
So she can't handle this

CHORUS 2: Furry soft cuddles?

CHORUS 1: My bulbs and wires hum
Louder. Louder.
Closer. Closer.
Like a tell-tale heart.
Whose heart is it?

ERICA: How is this hurting Kevin?
Everyone wins
For some insane reason he likes me
I guess he can have me
Part of me, at least
Just enough for Trish
And just enough for himself
And just enough for everyone else
And I'll still get my own heart for myself
And nobody ever has to know
The secret language written there.

CHORUS 1: I push the shadows around

With my flickering light
They almost make a question mark

ERICA: I wouldn't know
I've never dated anyone before
Kevin, he…
He doesn't make me feel like I want to turn into a
statue
So that's good, I guess

CHORUS 3: Open
See the way I spread myself to you
Inviting your fingers in
Your face
Feel me against your skin
So, so lightly
Can you touch him like that?

ERICA: If he wants to
Then I guess I'll have to try
How bad can it be, right?
To feel someone with my skin
Kevin
To touch him with my lips
People do it all the time
And I'm a person
And he's a person.
(*She touches her own face.*)
We're made of the same cells
(*She kisses her own arm.*)
That's not so bad
I can do this
I have to call him
Tomorrow. No. Tonight.
And I can do this
I can do this

I can do this....

(KEVIN's *apartment. Bottom line, it's the kind of place a guy
like him can afford, even in a town like this, A K A crappy.
We see, prominently displayed somewhere, the following:
several grinning skeletons and other Dia de los Muertos
memorabilia, several colorful shot glasses bearing the
names of international cities, and a row of fantasy-themed
figurines.)*

KEVIN: Well, here we are.

(ERICA *is silent.)*

KEVIN: It's not Versailles or anything, but I've done my
best with the place.

(ERICA *is silent.)*

KEVIN: Oh God. You hate it. It's a dump, I know.

ERICA: What? Oh. No. You just, um, have a lot of stuff.

KEVIN: Oh, yeah. I kind of like to collect things. I think
of it as lowbrow eclectic kitsch. I know it sounds
shallow and materialistic, but my collections remind
me who I am. That sounds really stupid when you say
it out loud.

ERICA: No, I get it. I...completely get it. And I...I think
it's really cool that you...feel that way. Objects remind
me who I am all the time. Um. So where'd you get all
of it?

KEVIN: The Dia de los Muertos stuff mostly came from
a shop in Framingham. The D & D figurines are from
when I was a kid.

ERICA: What about the shot glasses?

KEVIN: I got the first one when I went Montreal
six years ago. I thought that would be my thing...
travel the world, bring back a shot glass from each
destination. I haven't exactly traveled much since then,

so they sort of represent the places I'm going to visit, some day.

*(He puts on music.)*

You want a glass of wine, or…?

ERICA: A glass of water would be great. Or maybe some juice or something?

KEVIN: I've got orange. The really good shit, with lots of that pulpy stuff in it. You OK with pulpy stuff?

ERICA: Love it.

KEVIN: Cool. Be right back.

*(KEVIN exits. As he does, the CHORUS enters.)*

ERICA: Um. Hi.

CHORUS 1: My painted metal bones

Lean in toward you.

ERICA: Yes, I can hear you, but this isn't really—

CHORUS 2: Let's fly away, m'lady

On my little plastic scaly wings!

ERICA: No offense, but I'm here to see Kevin. I can't—

CHORUS 3: Look inside my smooth curve!

I wanna get you druuuuunk!

ERICA: I get it, you're lonely, but that's just—

*(The CHORUS begins repeating their lines in chaotically overlapping fashion.)*

ERICA: Okay, that…could you…not all at once….SHUT UP!

KEVIN: *(Voice only)* One glass of orange juice for the lady, extra pulpy. I swear, you'll be picking bits out of your teeth for weeks.

*(The CHORUS exits. KEVIN enters with a glass of juice and sits back down.)*

KEVIN: You sure you don't want to go to a movie or a restaurant or something?

ERICA: Why would I want to do that?

KEVIN: You. Me. Here, at Chateau Kevin. I just want to make sure you don't think things are moving too, I don't know, fast.

ERICA: Why? Do you?

KEVIN: As long as you're comfortable, I'm comfortable.

ERICA: I'm comfortable. Super comfortable

KEVIN: Good.

(KEVIN *puts an arm around* ERICA. *With considerable effort, she stays within his embrace.*)

ERICA: So are you feeling any better? You know, since your birthday.

KEVIN: I dunno. I've been thinking about the whole aborted move to Waltham thing. Why I choked.

ERICA: Come to any conclusions?

KEVIN: I think it's just…if I leave this place, and I'm still totally miserable, then the problem has to be me, right? And, you know, then what? What about you? Don't you ever think about getting the hell out of here?

ERICA: I don't know. Where would I go?

KEVIN: *Anywhere.* Me, I have this picture of myself in some city. Maybe Boston. Maybe New York. Working on my novel. And I'll belong. I've…I've never really had that before.

ERICA: Your novel? That's…that's really great. What's it about?

KEVIN: Witches. But not, like, in a trashy way. There's this guy-guy witch couple and…it's sort of social commentary, really. The best genre fiction always is. The whole witch thing is sort of a metaphor for

frustration oppressed people feel. I dunno. I hear
myself, and I hear how stupid all this sounds….

ERICA: I'd love to read it some day.

KEVIN: What about you, Erica?

ERICA: What about me?

KEVIN: What do you want? Where do you see yourself?
What do you dream about? Sorry, that was the corniest
thing I've probably ever said. Forget—

ERICA: Being understood. That's what I dream about.

KEVIN: I'd like to think I'm on my way to some kind of
understanding.

ERICA: I mean…somebody seeing me. Really seeing
me. Every part. And still understanding.

KEVIN: Well, let me just put it out there, that I have
done more than a little over sharing with you, so
you're welcome to return the favor. Any time.

ERICA: Thanks. I'll keep that in mind.

KEVIN: What about getting out of here? If you could
live anywhere in the world, anywhere at all, where
would it be? Quick, answer without thinking.

ERICA: I, um…

KEVIN: Without thinking. Right now. Go.

ERICA: North Adams. The Berskhires.

KEVIN: Curveball.

ERICA: Mom and I spent the weekend in the Berkshires
two years ago. Right after she was diagnosed. It was
the only trip we ever took together…like, just the two
of us. And what I remember most is how quiet it was. I
remember feeling…happy there.

KEVIN: I took you for more of a Cambridge kind of gal.

ERICA: I don't really…do cities. The noise. Everything trying to talk to you. I mean, everyone.

KEVIN: North Adams. Okay, okay. I can get behind this. Tanglewood. Shakespeare and Company. Solid choice.

ERICA: I don't mean I—

KEVIN: Totally hypothetical. All of this. I…like to daydream. That's all. The daydream's just a little nicer with you in it.

(KEVIN *looks* ERICA *right in the eyes. She makes a huge effort to meet his gaze.*)

KEVIN: Would it be alright if I kissed you?

ERICA: Okay.

(KEVIN *does.*)

KEVIN: I kind of can't believe this is happening.

ERICA: Neither can I.

KEVIN: Full disclosure, I've sort of been nursing this crush on you for oh, I don't know, fifteen years or so.

ERICA: What? Why?

KEVIN: Give yourself a little more credit, Erica.

ERICA: I…I don't know what to say.

KEVIN: The only thing you have to say is that I can kiss you again.

ERICA: Okay.

(KEVIN *kisses* ERICA *again. He touches her, tentatively. She shrinks from his touch.*)

KEVIN: Erica? Are you…are you okay?

ERICA: Yeah.

KEVIN: You don't…I mean…you *have* done this before, right? (*Less jokingly*) Right?

ERICA: Yes!, Yes, of course, I…why'd you stop? What you were doing, that was…nice.

KEVIN: Well I do value feedback. Just putting it out there.

ERICA: Are you still here?
I need you now
Would you….?
Say something, please

KEVIN: Of course I'm here. I need you too…

(CHORUS 1 *enters.*)

CHORUS 1: Look, just look

At the articulated metal of my bones
Think, just think
Of the sound I'd make
If you shook me
So, so gently.

ERICA: Oh. Shit. Oh. Um.

(CHORUS 1 *exits.*)

KEVIN: Was that…are you okay? Should I—

ERICA: No. Don't stop.

(CHORUS 2 *enters.*)

CHORUS 2: Imagine, m'lady,

Fire breathing out of my little plastic mouth
And onto your neck
The phantom sensation
Warming your body
Kindling something inside of you

KEVIN: What is it? What's wrong? Do I need to brush my teeth? What?

(CHORUS 2 *exits.*)

ERICA: No. It's me. Sorry. I—

KEVIN: We can—

ERICA: *No!* How…how do you like that?

KEVIN: Mmmm. Very nice.

ERICA: I need you. Stay with me.

(CHORUS 3 *enters.*)

CHORUS 3: What would it be like

To trace your finger
Along the perfect swooping edge
Of my rim?
Think of how smooth I'd be
How perfectly arched I am
Commune with—

(ERICA *cries out.* CHORUS 3 *exits.*)

KEVIN: Okay, that's…this is clearly not okay. *You're* clearly not okay. I—

ERICA: Please don't stop

KEVIN: Hey. Erica. Look at me. *Look* at me.

ERICA: I'm sorry. I thought I could. I thought—

KEVIN: Did… Did I do something wrong?

ERICA: No. I…I can't really talk about it. Okay?

KEVIN: I sort of feel like we *have* to talk about it. I mean, if I hurt you, or—are you leaving?

ERICA: I'm sorry.

KEVIN: Hold up. I need to—

ERICA: I have to go. I have to—

KEVIN: You can't just—

ERICA: It's not your fault. I'm sorry.

(ERICA *exits.* KEVIN *looks after her and sighs. He exits and* DEE *enters, followed shortly by* ERICA. *She looks at him in silence for a moment.*)

ERICA: I'm sorry

DEE: A stillness in the air
An absence of sound
My electricity changes to a frequency
Silent to your ears.

ERICA: I know why you're mad
I get it
But I wasn't trying to reject you, or us
I just…wanted to feel something for Kevin too
Not instead of you, just…
For both of you
It would be a lot easier for me if I did

DEE: Nothingness radiates
I lean away from you

ERICA: Hang on, that's the thing
As soon as he touched me
As soon as I touched him…
His skin was already a little sticky with sweat
And I could feel muscles moving under skin
And all I could think was…I was wrong
I can't…I was wrong…I…
How do people *enjoy* this?
And things were throbbing
Which is such a weird and horrible sensation
Like a heartbeat turned into something threatening
And our bodies were sticking together
And—

DEE: Blink. Flicker. Fizzle.
Welcome to iry Queen
(*He closes his eyes.*)

ERICA: Dee?

(DEE *is silent.*)

ERICA: *Dee?*

(DEE *exits. The sign is now half burnt-out.*)

ERICA: I'm sorry
I'm done with all this
The pretending, the lying
So you can come back now, okay?
(*Silence*)
Say something, Dee.
(*Silence. Silence*)
Please, just say something. Please....
(*Transition. Time passes.*)
I have an image in my mind
Mr Martinson's desk, ninth grade,
And just staring, staring, staring.
I barely passed that class
Because all I did was stare
And one day Kim Andre and Jessica Walters
Descended on me after class.
And Kim was like...don't think we haven't seen you
staring
And Jessica was like...oh, you are bad
But there was a certain...camaraderie in what they
were saying
And I had this huge feeling of relief
Someone else understands how I'm feeling
But then they kept on talking
And I realized what they really meant
Because...you remember everyone had these major
crushes on Mr. Martinson, right?
(*The light widens.* ERICA *is sitting with* KEVIN, *in the Dairy
Queen parking lot.*)

KEVIN: And this has…what, exactly to do with you running out on me last night?

ERICA: I'm getting there
I wasn't staring at him
Mr Martinson, I mean
I was staring at the stapler on his desk
And the next day I looked up there again
And I thought…Mr Martinson, not the stapler
Mr Martinson, not the stapler
And day after day, I could not stop thinking about that stapler
So one day I…
I stole it, the stapler
And kept it in my bed
And this is going to sound really weird
But I felt it reaching out to me
And that stapler didn't leave my room for two years
And that…that was the beginning I guess

KEVIN: If this is your idea of a joke, or….

ERICA: I'm not joking. I swear.

KEVIN: A *stapler*?

ERICA: This is…this is really hard for me. Could you… could you let me finish? Then you can ask anything you want and say anything you want.

KEVIN: Fine. Fair enough.

ERICA: So eventually…after the stapler, I mean
I realized that I was more into big things
Towering things
Like, for a good five years I spent most of my nights in the gazebo down in Cook's Park
It felt so…nice to be surrounded like that
It felt safe
And it also felt….well, other things too

That's the reason I didn't go off to college, you know
I couldn't take the gazebo with me if I did....
And the whole time, I'm thinking to myself...
I just like beautiful things
But at the back of my head, over all these years
Is Mr Martinson's stapler
And the things that went through my head when I
thought that Kim and Jessica were staring at it too
But I tell myself...it doesn't mean anything
*It doesn't mean anything*
And then, I met Dee
The Dairy Queen Sign, I mean
One night, six months ago, I got a flat tire
And pulled into the parking lot at night
And found myself under his glow
And looked up at him, and just thought...wow
And it's funny, because I had seen him before
Ten thousand times
There isn't a moment when something amazing
becomes amazing
It's just amazing
The thing that has to change is you
And your ability to see.
So after that, it got a lot harder to say that it doesn't
mean anything
Because I was in love
That's why I started coming by so much
To be with Dee
I finally admitted it to myself
It was only a week ago
But it feels about a hundred years
I told Dee, I love you
And he told me he loved me back
And the next day at work

I stopped ignoring the world around me and said hello
And that…that's what happened that first day we
talked out here
So…I'm done now, I guess.

(KEVIN *just stares at* ERICA.)

ERICA: Say something…please

KEVIN: So you're telling me that you talk to staplers
and signs and shit. And they talk back to you. That's
some next-level—

ERICA: No. No. I don't think they're actually speaking
words to me. I sense them. But sometimes I really talk
back. More and more lately.

KEVIN: And, what, they told you to run out on me last
night?

ERICA: I'm not used to that sort of thing with…with
people. I just got a little freaked out.

KEVIN: Right. You're more used to…*Dee*. The love of
your life is the Dairy Queen Sign.

ERICA: Well…yeah.

KEVIN: Because of the way the light hits you.

ERICA: Not just that. But yeah.

KEVIN: That light hits, like, dozens of people on a
nightly basis.

ERICA: Sure. And I touch lots of objects every day.
Monogamy's kind of impossible in a relationship like
this, so we don't really get hung up on it.

KEVIN: I just don't…I can't even process this right now.
It's so fucked up.

ERICA: Um. So Dee is, well he's not himself right
now. Obviously. I guess…I guess I was wondering…
if they're planning on fixing him. Or if you could,
maybe—

KEVIN: Why do you keep saying him?

ERICA: I don't know. Dee's a him.

KEVIN: Does he have a dick somewhere that I haven't seen?

ERICA: No. His...his energy is male. I can sense it. And he...I mean his energy is...it's beautiful. And with him burnt out like this...it's sad. If you could please...*please* Kevin, just help him...it would mean a lot to me.

KEVIN: You want to break up with me. I get that. Just... be honest with me, okay? You don't have to pull this bullshit.

ERICA: If I was going to make up some lie to break up with you...don't you think I'd come up with something a little easier?

(KEVIN *considers this.*)

KEVIN: I guess so. But—

ERICA: I'm telling you this because you deserve the truth. And because...you seemed like maybe you might...I dunno. Get it.

KEVIN: So, what, you fuck them in some way? The stapler? The gazebo? *Dee?*

ERICA: It's not sex in the way you'd think of sex...it's mostly...touching. Rubbing. That sort of thing.

KEVIN: Okay, I...why am I even continuing this conversation? I should go.

ERICA: Kevin, I...

(ERICA *trails off.* KEVIN *looks up at the sign and thinks.*)

KEVIN: Okay, I...I was seeing this therapist for a while, over in Milford. And he was great. I don't know if this kind of thing is even in his wheelhouse, but...just go see him. Once. Tell him everything—

ERICA: I don't—

KEVIN: If you can't, you know, afford it…I have some cash saved up. For the big move to wherever. So if you need me to spot you, I really don't mind. At this point, what's another year stuck in this town, am I right?

ERICA: That's a very generous offer.

KEVIN: Cool. Great. I—

ERICA: Bye, Kevin.

KEVIN: Oh. Yeah. Okay. Bye, then.

ERICA: Please see what you can do about getting the sign fixed, okay? It's not his fault.

KEVIN: Nothing can be the sign's fault, Erica. It's just a sign.

(KEVIN *exits. The scene shifts to* ERICA's *bedroom. With her left hand, she switches the lamp on and off, over and over again. In her right hand, she holds the can opener. The teddy bear sits in her lap.* TRISH *appears on the other side of the door and knocks.*)

TRISH: Erica? Come on, open up. *(pause)* Still sick? If there's any way you can, you know, pull yourself together…I mean, you're still new, so three days is kind of a lot to…right. I'm not going to mother you. *(pause)* Well, I ordered a pizza, so come on out later, if you're feeling hungry. *(pause)* I guess I'll let you get some rest….
*(She exits.)*

ERICA: I just keep running through every moment in my head
What else could I have said
What else could I have done?

*(The* CHORUS *enters.)*

CHORUS 2: Floppy sad arms!
Sinking down!

ERICA: Remember when I'd hold onto you
When I missed my dad?
You always made me feel better
Well I'm holding onto you right now
So make me feel better.

CHORUS 1: Pop!
My bulb crackles
Making spots in your eyes
Each one of them, an accusation.

ERICA: I thought he might understand
I was wrong

CHORUS 3: Open
Smoothly, gently, slowly
Thrusting myself right into the sky
Like a signpost

ERICA: I haven't forgotten about Dee
I just don't know what to do

CHORUS 1: My light
Burning through the shade
Feel it
And remember the only thing you have left.

ERICA: But I ruined things with Dee

CHORUS 2: My eyes!
So shiny! So smooth!
Look!
Follow them!
Out the door! Past the house!
Up the street! Keep going!
Go! Go!
You know where.

ERICA: I…
You're right

Even if he's still upset
I can't give up

CHORUS 3: Listen, very closely
The creak of my hinge
What did it say?

ERICA: Dee…
I'll fix him, somehow
I won't leave him
Not until he's bright and shining again
And maybe then he'll understand…
What?
That I love him
That I need him
That I'm sorry.

*(The* CHORUS *exits and* DEE *enters.)*

DEE: The air sparkles with my luminance
Feel the pulse of my energy
Feel it tingle on your face
That's me, caressing you.

ERICA: You're back
You're…
Does this mean you forgive me?

DEE: The hum in the air is back
A signal I'm broadcasting to you
Step into my light
It matches your eyes tonight
Radiating
Radiating
Radiating

ERICA: You saved me all over again
It's like that first time
That first day

Your light touching me
Pulling me back from the edge

KEVIN: *(Voice)* All I really expected was a thank you. But then again, I have always said flattery will get you everywhere. So please, do go on....

(KEVIN *appears. He and* ERICA *are underneath the Dairy Queen Sign, which is now fully lit.*)

ERICA: Kevin...

KEVIN: Yo.

(ERICA *looks back and forth from the sign to* KEVIN.)

KEVIN: I do believe I said go on.

ERICA: Did you...?

(KEVIN *bows.*)

ERICA: How?

KEVIN: Not to undersell myself or anything, but I *am* practically a manager.

ERICA: But why would you...I mean, aren't you....

KEVIN: I hate to see you sad.

ERICA: So are you still pissed?

KEVIN: It's just that...okay, I get that I was essentially the test subject, but you really need to work on your sales pitch.

ERICA: My "sales pitch"?

KEVIN: Well, for starters, you could use the actual lingo.

ERICA: What...lingo?

KEVIN: Don't even tell me you haven't tried googling this stuff before.

ERICA: Of course I did. Of course. Years ago. Before googling was even a thing. I think I asked Jeeves...

KEVIN: And?

ERICA: And the first result I got was the web site called "A Guide to The World's Weirdest and Freakiest Fetishes:". I didn't really want to see any more after that.

KEVIN: So you really never looked up any other…I mean, you don't know—

ERICA: Look, I really don't care if you think I'm just some freak with a weird fetish. I don't care if you think I'm crazy. I—

(KEVIN *takes out a tablet or phone and shows it to* ERICA.)

ERICA: Here. Check it out.
(*She reads out loud from the screen.*)
"Welcome to Objectum Sexuality International".

KEVIN: And here. Click on that. They have a message board. Look…this woman here? She loves flags. Says that they're silly and flirty. She's in a committed relationship with the welcome flag on the front of her house. That's cute, right? And this guy here…he's into buttons. It's like what you said about…monogamy. He says it too. I mean, how many buttons do you touch over the course of the day? And here—

ERICA: What?

KEVIN: A link to create a new profile. On the message board, I mean.

ERICA: I don't think I can—

KEVIN: I do. I think you can.

ERICA: Why are you being so cool about this?

KEVIN: Why wouldn't I be?

ERICA: I can think of at least a dozen reasons. Number one, I kind of put you in a—

KEVIN: Okay. Um. Before. You asked why I like you. And I have this...memory of you, in homeroom. That purple hair. The long black skirt you always wore. And Kim and Jessica were throwing pencils at you...and you were just staring out the window. I saw your face, and it was just...somewhere else. Total Zen.

ERICA: Oh. Yeah. I had a major thing for the streetlight out in the parking lot.

KEVIN: Well, I...that expression made everything about you transcend. It was like...here's someone who doesn't give a shit about Kim or Jessica or homecoming or prom or...she's just *her*. And...you remember how much shit I got from Joe and Marc. But I looked at you and...and the image of you by that window has been this reminder to not give a shit. For all these years. So when I judged you like that, all I could think afterwards was...I'm Kim. I'm Jessica. I'm Joe. I'm Marc. I'm every other asshole in this town, bringing you down. I let my feelings get in the way.//And hey—

ERICA: Oh, Kevin, you—

KEVIN: —Who am I or anyone to judge? You and Dee seem...well, you're lucky. Lucky to have each other. I'd be kind of a piece of shit for hating on other people's happiness, right? I guess what I mean is... congratulations, you know? For being you. It's not easy, especially in a town like this.

ERICA: Thanks, Kevin. Really. I...thank you.

(KEVIN *hands the phone/tablet to* ERICA.)

KEVIN: So go on. This is your big moment. I mean, I'm not going to drumroll this shit or anything, but...just go on.

ERICA: I wouldn't know what to say....

KEVIN: Other people kind of tell their stories. Talk about their relationships. That kind of thing.

(ERICA *thinks, then begins typing on the tablet.* DEE *enters.*)

ERICA: I feel...what?
Light, floating
But not outside my body
I'm here, whole
Somewhere in the sky.

DEE: Feel my base
The friction of its little pits and bumps
That's me, touching you back

ERICA: It's like I can see you from a new angle
Way up here
Touch your letters
Or see you with more...perspective I guess
This is real
My hand on you is real
The process of diffusion, cooling my skin to the same
temperature of your base
That's real
The way the sky and the air and the whole world is
different under your light
That's the most real thing.
DEE: I shine on you
Somehow, the shadows go away
And the only thing that exists
Is my light
Everything is made of light

(*The scene shifts to* TRISH *and* ERICA's *house.*)

ERICA: Trish? Trish, you around? There's something I
need to talk to you about...

(ERICA *has a thought, and turns the T V on.*)

T V VOICE: You're watching Channel 47, Blackstone Valley Cable Access, bringing you live election night coverage.

ERICA: Wait, it's…what's today? Shit.

(FRANK *enters.*)

FRANK: Just to recap, the "yes" side has been declared victorious for Ballot Question 6, also known as the Downtown Revitalization Bill. I'm here at Town Hall, where Selectwoman Trish Grillo, author of the legislation, is about to hold a press conference.

TRISH: Thank you. Thank you. Yes. Oh, hi Frank. I see you! Thank you. Thank you all! Friends, this isn't just my victory today. It's yours. It's your neighbor's. This victory belongs to the entire town!

This is a new day for our little community. And I don't know about you, but I am so excited for the future.

Here's what I'm thinking, friends: I'm thinking we can be a trend-setter. Our little town can be a model for the entire region. Imagine that. Us. And that's thanks to the Downtown Revitalization Bill. That's thanks to all of you.

And as part of our big dream, our ambition to transform towns and cities across Massachusetts and bring our fractured communities back together, it's time to take the next step in our revolution. I am officially announcing my run for State Senate.

(*Applause.* TRISH *smiles and waves for a moment, then crosses to join* ERICA.)

ERICA: Hey. How was the party?

TRISH: Exciting. Amazing. I missed you.

ERICA: I watched the broadcast. It was just—

TRISH: Too much for you. I get it. I'm not mad.

ERICA: Okay, so—

TRISH: What I am, though, is beat. So I'm just going to—

ERICA: Please don't go to bed yet. Please. I just want want to—say a couple of things.

TRISH: What? What is it?

ERICA: Okay. Um, well first of all…I'm really proud of you. You've worked so hard for this…for all of this. And uh…I just wanted to make sure I said that to you. Because I know I don't say things like that enough. And I mean it. And I do appreciate everything you've done. Since Mom died. Letting me stay with you, and…well, everything.

TRISH: Well of course. That's what family's for, right?

ERICA: Right, yeah. And…I told you I've been working on myself lately. Since Mom. And I think I've finally figured some stuff out. It's like…I'm finally seeing everything I was missing before. And it's so beautiful that I just…I couldn't not tell you about it. God, I don't even really know what I'm supposed to say next. Okay, I met someone I want to tell you all about him. His name is Dee.

TRISH: Dee? What about Kevin?

ERICA: I lied to you about that. Sort of. It's complicated.

TRISH: I knew it! I knew that kid was gay.

ERICA: He's not…focus, Trish, okay?

TRISH: Fine. Who is this Dee?

ERICA: He's…a sign.

TRISH: A sign of what?

ERICA: No, I mean like literally. Dee is the Dairy Queen sign. The sign itself. That's…that's who I met.

TRISH: I don't understand.

ERICA: I'm...I'm objectum sexual, Trish. That means...
I'm not attracted to men. Or women. Or people at all.
I'm attracted to...to inanimate objects. I know it's a
lot, but I have some information about it, if you want.
It's—

TRISH: Oh, haha, very funny. I remember. I saw that
weird sex show on TLC last month. That woman who
was humping fence posts or whatever. You got me. I
have to say, I like this side of you. You've never had a
sense of humor before.

ERICA: I'm not. I'm not kidding.

TRISH: Sure.

ERICA: I've actually been talking to the woman from
that TLC show online, and she's really nice, and smart.
She's so well-spoken about why we love our objects,
and what it's like. The network decided to just show
like two minutes of her being affectionate with her
fence and none of the other stuff. That's not usually
what it's like.

TRISH: Okay, very convincing, but you can drop it now,
alright?

ERICA: There's nothing to drop. This isn't a joke. I'm
telling you something important about my life. This is
who I am.

*(For once, TRISH is speechless.)*

ERICA: There's a web site, with a lot of really helpful
info, if you want to find out more. You know, about
who I am. It's called—

TRISH: I just...

ERICA: What? What is it?

TRISH: I just...can't.

*(She abruptly exits.)*

ERICA: Trish? Trish?

(KEVIN *enters. Scene shifts to the Dairy Queen parking lot.*)

KEVIN: Hey. Just breathe. It's alright. You did great. Really.

ERICA: Then why isn't she answering her phone, Kevin?

KEVIN: It's kind of a lot to process, right? That's what she's doing. Processing.

ERICA: I...I never should have told her. What the hell was I thinking? I...I—

KEVIN: Hey now. Calm down. Don't panic. Did I ever tell you about coming out to my dad?

ERICA: No...

KEVIN: I never really thought I would. I just figured...I date a girl? Bring her home. I date a guy? That's between me and Dionysus.

ERICA: What is that? One of those hookup apps?

KEVIN: Greek god of hedonism. Sort of the prototypical pansexual. So anyhow, I started seeing this Australian guy from a D & D game. And that fucker actually gave me an ultimatum: come out to your dad or it's over. He was like, (*Bad Australian accent*) "I refuse to be your dirty little secret". So yeah, I mean, that accent...I just...told him...okay Dad, I'm seeing someone. His name is Max. And for a second there, he thought I was telling him I was gay, which he was oddly cool with. But I tried to explain that I don't like labels, and gender's not such a big deal to me...and for some reason that really set him off. He actually said to me, "What, so you'll just sleep with anything that moves?"

ERICA: He didn't.

KEVIN: Oh, but he did. To which I said, "Well, that brings us to my necrophilia." Once I got him to stop shouting for long enough to tell him I was just kidding…things eased up a bit. Not that things weren't weird between us for, I dunno, a couple years…but we got there. Sometimes it just takes a little time. And the threat of necrophilia…

ERICA: What ever happened to the Australian guy?

KEVIN: Dumped me for a minotaur like a week later. But the point is, it was all good, and I'm glad it happened. My dad and I are totally great now. It just took a little time.

ERICA: Kevin, that's…at least your dad had a frame of reference for who you are. There've been parades, court cases, characters on T V shows. My sister just thinks I'm some mentally ill pervert.

KEVIN: But I don't think that.

ERICA: Thanks.

KEVIN: I'm serious. No matter what your sister or anyone else in this town thinks, I'm here, and I think you're amazing.

(ERICA *takes* KEVIN's *hand. He looks down at their entwined hands, then pulls away.*)

ERICA: I think you're amazing too

KEVIN: This is…I know you're not doing it on purpose. It's, like, a really confusing stressful time for you. I get it. But this whole thing has been very, very hard for me to wrap my head around and accept. And I mean this in the least bitchy way possible when I say…don't toy with me, Erica.

ERICA: I'm not. I've been thinking about this a lot. Dee and I were never exclusive. I've been talking to the people on the message board. And I told them about you, and how amazing and fantastic you've been, and how much I care about you. And…turns out, that's not so weird for O S people. They all have their objects, but a lot of them have people too. And the relationships are different. But they all matter.

KEVIN: I think you're talking about friends.

ERICA: No, I'm not. One person. Someone you align with. Spiritually.

KEVIN: Are you sexually attracted to me?

ERICA: What?

KEVIN: It's not a complicated question. Are you sexually attracted to me?

ERICA: That doesn't matter.

KEVIN: To you. It doesn't matter to you. What if it matters to me?

ERICA: The way the people on the message board explained it...what if...we have each other. And I have Dee. And sometimes other things too. You know. Just for fun.

KEVIN: Like the can opener.

ERICA: Yeah. Like the can opener. And you can have other people when you want to. Guys. Girls. Whatever. That way everyone gets what they want. So...what do you think?

(KEVIN *hesitates. A* CHORUS *member enters, also in a Dairy Queen uniform. This is* JULIE. TRISH *follows her. They're in mid-conversation, and don't see* Erica *and* KEVIN *at first.*)

TRISH: Well I'm so glad you've come around on the Downtown Revitalization Project, Julie.
(*She pulls a check out of her briefcase.*)
Demolition has to start within two weeks of you cashing this. Part of the whole program. Is that going to be a problem?

JULIE: Naw, I'm a franchisee. Basically means I get to be a little Napoleon and do whatever the hell I want. I'll let corporate know but yeah, we're golden.

TRISH: And the sign?

JULIE: Huh? What about the sign?

TRISH: That's being replaced too?

JULIE: Eh. I'll probably leave the base and just replace the top part. Save some cash.

TRISH: The sign has to be replaced too. The whole thing. Or no deal.

JULIE: Jesus Christ. You wanna pick out the toilet seats too?

TRISH: Do we have a deal?

JULIE: Fine. Deal.

(JULIE *and* TRISH *shake hands.* TRISH *hands* JULIE *the check.*)

ERICA: Trish? What the hell is going on?

KEVIN: A shadowy backroom deal? In our little town? I feel so cosmopolitan.

JULIE: Russell. Grillo. Your ten was supposed to be over…four and half minutes ago. What are you still doing out here?

ERICA: What the fuck is this, Trish?

JULIE: Well, this is as good a time as any to tell you you're fired.

TRISH: Well, I'd better get back to Town Hall.

ERICA: No! No! You are not going anywhere until you tell me why the fuck you're doing this! What did Dee ever do to you?!

TRISH: Will you lower your voice?

ERICA: Wouldn't want anyone to hear, right? Wouldn't want anyone to make a scene. That's all you care about. That's all you've ever cared about!

JULIE: So. Just to be clear, once I cash this, the town can't take it back, right?

TRISH: That's right, but—

JULIE: Well, I've got fifteen minutes until Rockland Bank closes, so…good luck with whatever the hell all this is.
(*She exits.*)

ERICA: Trish. Please, listen to me. Dee, he's—

TRISH: I don't want to hear about your sick fetishes, Erica. I'm your sister. It's…gross.

KEVIN: See, that's a common misconception, but the sexual aspect of these relationships is actually—

ERICA: Kevin. Please.

KEVIN: Butting out. Right-o.

TRISH: Just tell me. You've been humping that sign, the way your friend on T V does with her fence?

ERICA: Sometimes. And I'm not ashamed of it. But it's about so much more than—

TRISH: Really, Erica that's—for one thing, it's not sanitary. Think of how many dogs have probably pissed on that sign.

ERICA: So what, I should fuck a guy instead? Dicks are the literal source of pee. Try again.

TRISH: This is clearly some sort of reaction. To Mom's death. You're looking for, I don't know, attention, or—

ERICA: It's not! You think this is something new I just decided to try out for the hell of it? I have felt this way my whole life. But I just…couldn't before. It was always something inside me, but I guess I didn't want

Mom to be disappointed in me, you know? But now that I'm...me, really me, I'd like to think she could have understood. And that maybe you still can, too.

TRISH: What I'm trying to understand is what's at the root of all this. And how I can help you.

ERICA: One thing that's not going to help me is tearing down the entire Dairy Queen.

TRISH: See, I think you're wrong about that. Once you're not...humping up on that thing anymore, your head is going to clear and you're going to be you again. It's a scientific fact. Endorphins or something. I saw an article on Facebook.

ERICA: Please, Trish. Please. Don't kill Dee just to prove some kind of point. Please.

TRISH: Listen to the words that are coming out of your mouth. It's a sign. You can't kill it because it's not alive.

ERICA: Then what about you, and your career? Huh? The Downtown Revitalization Project is supposed to be for small businesses. You're breaking your campaign promises. People are going to be pissed.

TRISH: I don't care.

ERICA: You'd really risk your whole run for state senate?

TRISH: Yeah. I would.

ERICA: That doesn't make any goddamn sense.

TRISH: I promised Mom I would take care of you.

ERICA: Then call off the demolition, okay? That's the best way you can take care of me.

TRISH: I'm not going to do that. Part of taking care of a person is doing hard things that you know are for the best. I hope you understand that? We'll fix this. We'll figure it out. Together.

ERICA: No. We won't. Because you will never see me again after this. Never. You understand?

TRISH: Erica, you don't—

ERICA: Bye, Trish.

*(She turns away from* TRISH *to look up at* DEE.*)*

TRISH: Erica? Look at me. Please. Please…okay, we'll talk later. Once you've had a chance to…calm down. I love you, alright?
*(She exits.)*

DEE: My light blinks on
And wavers just a little.
In that slight hesitation
An acknowledgment

KEVIN: Hey, are you okay?

DEE: Transferring energy
Vibrations,
Invisible things
Emptying myself to fortify you

KEVIN: This is total bullshit. We're not going to let them get away with this. We'll…do…something…

ERICA: No. It's too late. He knows it, too. It's too late. It's too late…

DEE: Constant, solid
I don't waver in front of you
I remain stoic in the night

KEVIN: Uh…hey buddy. We're going to do everything we can to help you, okay?

ERICA: He would never let me worry about him
That's the way he is
He's brave

KEVIN: You are too, Erica.

(ERICA, KEVIN, *and* DEE *exit. Three members of the chorus enters and become message board posters.*)

MESSAGE BOARD POSTER 1: I understand what you're going through. My lover was torn down, years ago. I watched it happen. And not only were people indifferent, they celebrated.

ERICA: What? Why would people do something like that?

MESSAGE BOARD POSTER 1: A lot of people did not care for him.

ERICA: Why not? Who was he?

MESSAGE BOARD POSTER 1: The Berlin Wall.

ERICA: *(To herself)* Shit.

MESSAGE BOARD POSTER 2: I promise you, Dee is so much more worried about you than he is about himself. The way you've described him, Dee sounds pretty stoic to me.

ERICA: But he's going to die.

MESSAGE BOARD POSTER 3: The First Law of Thermodynamics says that matter can neither be created nor destroyed. So if I cut up my dining room table into pieces, and use the wood to make two chairs instead, does some essence of the original table survive?

ERICA: I guess so.

MESSAGE BOARD POSTER 1: Gene's right. I go to visit him. The bits of the wall that now live in museums. I'm not saying that it's the same. But the basic essence of him endures. In some way, at least.

ERICA: I moved out of my sister's house. I've been staying with Kevin. I haven't even talked to her since... she did what she did. And I don't know what to do next.

MESSAGE BOARD POSTER 2: It sounds like what you need is a good beginning.

ERICA: Maybe. Probably. But I need one good ending first.

(KEVIN *and* DEE *and enter. Scene shifts back to the parking lot.*)

CHORUS 1: The vibrations in the air

CHORUS 2: The hum traveling between every single thing

CHORUS 3: The elegy of the universe

KEVIN: Does the sky look like a kind of weird color to you?

ERICA: It's red
Like Dee
Like his light.

KEVIN: Hey…careful where you…the sidewalk, it's all jack hammered to shit.

ERICA: It's okay
Those pieces down there, of pavement
They're protecting me
They won't let me fall

CHORUS 1: Shifting under your feet

KEVIN: Since when do random pieces of rubble talk to you?

ERICA: Everything's talking to me now

CHORUS 2: Sensing your forward motion

ERICA: All matter is basically the same, right?
It's not so weird when you remember that

CHORUS 3: Delivering you to him

ERICA: Dee, the ground, the bits of dust in the sky
And you

All part of one big continuum
Sending him off, together

DEE: I stand, calm and ready
My energy reaching into the night
The last gasp of it spilling all around you

KEVIN: You know something really weird? I think I...I
think I feel it too. I feel...something. Like someone put
pop rocks all over my skin and turned the hose on me.

DEE: Trying to sing to you
With my phantom electricity
I whisper it into your ear

CHORUS 1: And we echo it endlessly

CHORUS 2: Up into the sky

CHORUS 3: Into something eternal

KEVIN: Is he...still there?

ERICA: Here.

(ERICA *takes* KEVIN's *hand and guides it to* DEE.)

DEE: A tingle still buzzing
Somewhere inside of me

KEVIN: I don't really feel much.

ERICA: They disconnected his wiring this afternoon.
So....

CHORUS 1: Look, over here
At how I catch the light
And glimmer all the way over to you

KEVIN: Wait...holy shit.

ERICA: What?

KEVIN: I think my car just...talked to me.

CHORUS 2: Wrapped around you
I caress your arms, your back

I shelter you

KEVIN: Was that my shirt?

ERICA: It was, yeah
I felt it too

CHORUS 3: I hold you tight
A little tension in my touch
Squeezing you, right there

KEVIN: Um. My belt is definitely flirting with me

DEE: I quiver in the wind
Trying to be steady
Trying not to let you
See me falter.

KEVIN: Dee? Is that...?

ERICA: Yes
I just wish you could have met him
I mean, really met him
When he was himself
When he was glorious
When he was everything

KEVIN: Am I objectum-sexual now?

ERICA: I don't think so
Everything's just so much louder than usual tonight
The sky...the molecules...
You, me...Dee

KEVIN: Erica, what's going on? Why are we here?
DEE: I groan just a little
Where plastic meets metal
My morse code to you
My signal that I'm still here.

ERICA: Listen to me, Dee
You're going to fall

Try not to be afraid. It's going to be…
It's going to be beautiful, actually
You'll sail through the air
The mass and shape of you will whoosh
And cut the breeze
And make a little arc of red and white
You and the ground
Will feel each other in a new way
Think about how striking you'll look,
Right against the pavement like that, and…
And I'll be here
I promise
And when it's over I will take as many pieces of you as
I can
The things about you that made people so happy
I will take them and I will keep them
Forever

KEVIN: The construction guys aren't going to let you anywhere near here when they…you know.

ERICA: We're doing this tonight
It shouldn't be anyone else
He deserves to be treated gently
He deserves to be surrounded by love.

DEE: A headlight reflects off my surface
A reminder of before
A final gift to you

KEVIN: How are we going to do that? We don't have any equipment. We don't have any…whatever it is construction guys use to demolish signs.

(ERICA *pushes the sign.*)

DEE: I yield
To your touch

ERICA: They already jackhammered

He's loose
He's—

KEVIN: That's impossible. What you're saying it…it's not possible. It's a massive, several-ton sign.

ERICA: Impossible like communicating with your car
Or your shirt
Or your belt
Or Dee?

KEVIN: Yeah, but—

ERICA: He wants to
He's ready
He'll let go

DEE: I tilt, just a little
Just for you

KEVIN: I just…holy shit. Is this even happening?

ERICA: I think so.

KEVIN: Yeah. I think so too.

(*They look at each other.* ERICA *hesitates, then embraces* DEE.)

CHORUS 1: Everything, leaning in

CHORUS 2: Like the wind at your back

CHORUS 3: Pushing things to their conclusion

KEVIN: I think…I think it's working.

(DEE *leans back a bit.*)

DEE: Your hand
My pole
Together
Moving
As I lean in
To gravity
Feel it

(ERICA*'s embrace becomes aggressive.*)

KEVIN: Erica! Be careful...it's...I mean he's...I oh man...Jesus.

DEE: Scraping.
Grinding.
Tilting, tilting, tilting

(ERICA, *startled, momentarily disengages from* DEE.)

KEVIN: You've got this.

(ERICA *re-embraces* DEE *and leans in with all her might.*)

CHORUS 1: We're down below

CHORUS 2: Ready to catch you

CHORUS 3: Waiting to embrace you

ERICA: I'll be here the whole way.
Yes. I feel it too.
All of it. Yes. You can. You can.
You can. Yes.

KEVIN: Oh God—he's...he's actually—

DEE: Falling

CHORUS 1: Falling

CHORUS 2: Falling

CHORUS 3: Falling

(*The* CHORUS *quietly repeats "Falling" under the rest of the scene*)

KEVIN: Falling

ERICA: Falling
Falling
Falling
A perfect swoop

KEVIN: Falling

ERICA: A perfect arc

KEVIN: Falling

ERICA: A blur of color

KEVIN: Falling

ERICA: It's beautiful

(ERICA *gently kisses* DEE, *and lays him down on the ground. A giant crashing, splintering, smashing, thudding sound.* KEVIN *takes* ERICA*'s hand. Together, they look down on* DEE *whose eyes are closed. A moment, then* KEVIN *exits and the scene shifts Erica, alone in a different parking lot. A sign, reading "NORTH ADAMS MOTEL", flickers.* KEVIN *enters.*)

ERICA: That took a while.

KEVIN: Yeah. Sorry, I—

ERICA: We checked in?

KEVIN: Yeah, I think it's going to be pretty good. There's a kitchenette, and a little area with a desk and a couch, so it'll work. You know, until we can afford a real place.

ERICA: Great.

KEVIN: There's just, uh, one little thing.

(*A member of the* CHORUS, *dressed as a hotel desk clerk* [MIKE], *exits the motel. He puts a hand around* KEVIN*'s waist and drops a key into his hand.*)

MIKE: Mandy's going to cover for me. We have an hour. So…

ERICA: Is this the little thing?

KEVIN: Yeah. Um. Erica, this is Mike. Mike, Erica.

MIKE: Hi. Err. Is this your…?

KEVIN: Yeah. But she's cool.

ERICA: We both are. Cool, I mean.

MIKE: Whatever. Come on. Clock's ticking.

*(He exits.)*

KEVIN: You sure this is…?

ERICA: Two hundred percent sure. Go on. Have fun.

KEVIN: Hey. See that motel sign? The way he's flickering at you?

ERICA: I…may have noticed. And…it's a she.

KEVIN: Well I think *she's* winking at you.

*(KEVIN kisses ERICA and exits. A CHORUS member enters: the motel sign.)*

CHORUS 2: My light
Welcoming, inviting
My shape, like an arm
Waving hello.

ERICA: Oh. Hello, um…

*(ERICA touches the CHORUS member.)*

CHORUS 2: Feel the familiar solidity
Curving under your hand

*(ERICA pulls her hand back.)*

ERICA: I'm sorry.
I can't
Not yet
I…
*(She takes a large, jagged piece of red plastic out of her bag.)*
I want you to meet someone
This is Dee
You wouldn't know it by looking at him now
But Dee was quite the—

*(The CHORUS member exits. The motel sign has blinked off.)*

ERICA: Fine. Be that way.
*(She looks at the piece of plastic.)*
Are you…?

It's alright
I still feel you.

*(Silence. Silence. Silence. She touches the plastic. The motel sign flickers and blinks back on.* ERICA *looks up at it, then down at the piece of plastic. She holds it up so that the light of the motel sign shines through it.)*

ERICA: There
Look at you
With the light shining through you like that
It's almost like before
No…no, it's not
But just look at you shine
You're glowing
You're beautiful
You're perfect

## END OF PLAY

CPSIA information can be obtained
at www.ICGtesting.com
Printed in the USA
FSHW021944181120
75916FS